D1808613

# THE
# DEVIL'S
# GAUNTLET

The Church and the
Challenge of Society

## OS GUINNESS

INTERVARSITY PRESS
DOWNERS GROVE, ILLINOIS 60515

*InterVarsity Press is the book-publishing division of InterVarsity Christian Fellowship, a student movement active on campus at hundreds of universities, colleges and schools of nursing. For information about local and regional activities, write Public Relations Dept., InterVarsity Christian Fellowship, 6400 Schroeder Rd., P.O. Box 7895, Madison, WI 53707-7895.*

*Distributed in Canada through InterVarsity Press, 860 Denison St., Unit 3, Markham, Ontario L3R 4H1, Canada.*

*ISBN 0-8308-1108-7*

*Printed in the United States of America*

**Library of Congress Cataloging-in-Publication Data has been applied for.**

| 14 | 13 | 12 | 11 | 10 | 9 | 8 | 7 | 6 | 5 | 4 | 3 | 2 | 1 |
|----|----|----|----|----|---|---|---|---|---|---|---|---|---|
| 99 | 98 | 97 | 96 | 95 | 94 | 93 | 92 | 91 | 90 | 89 | | | |

Have you ever been in Eastern Europe and visited one of those countries where the militiamen go around in threes? The reason for it, it is said, is that the first one knows how to read, the second knows how to write, and the third is there to keep an eye on the other two dangerous intellectuals.

Many churches make us feel like that today. Speak intelligently for more than two minutes and with more than one thought in each, and you are considered dangerously intellectual and unspiritual. But the church today is beset by big problems and big issues, and these must be thought through carefully in light of the Word of God and the situation in our world today. We must forswear simple answers to tough questions and be prepared to pray, think and sweat intellectually in order to see where we are and what the Lord would have us to do.

One of the most momentous of these questions is this: How should the church today be related to society today? To set the context of this issue I will begin with a story and a quotation.

*The story:* Soviet leader Nikita Khrushchev used to tell of a time when there was a wave of petty theft in the Soviet Union. To curtail this the authorities put up guards around the factories. At one timberworks in Leningrad, the guard knew the workers in the factory very well. The first evening, out came Pyotr Petrovich with a wheelbarrow and, on the wheelbarrow, a great bulky sack with a suspicious-looking object inside.

"All right, Petrovich," said the guard, "what have you got there?"

"Oh, just sawdust and shavings," Petrovich replied.

"Come on," the guard said, "I wasn't born yesterday. Tip it out." And out came nothing but sawdust and shavings. So he was allowed to put it all back again and go home.

When the same thing happened every night of the week, the guard became frustrated. Finally, his curiosity overcame his frustration.

"Petrovich," he said, "I know you. Tell me what you're smuggling out of here, and I'll let you go."

"Wheelbarrows, my friend," said Petrovich, "wheelbarrows."

Laugh by all means, but when it comes to the issue of church and society the laugh is on us as evangelicals. We have set up patrols to check for secularism all around the country, and the devil has trundled secularization right past our own eyes and on into the church. We have conducted spot checks, looking for any conceivable lapse in biblical authority, and the devil has wheeled anarchy past the front doors of our homes and into our lifestyles.

Back in the early seventies, a professor at Oxford, knowing I was a Christian, asked me, "By the end of the seventies, who will be the worldliest Christians in America?" I must have looked a bit puzzled, so he went on, "I guarantee it will be the fundamentalists."

At the time that seemed startling. Worldliest? Fundamentalists then were world-denying by definition. But after 1987, a lamentable year of Christian scandal and shame, we hardly need to pause to answer that question. What has happened? One of the deepest reasons behind the corruption of evangelicalism and fundamentalism is a profound inadequacy in understanding how the church should engage society.

*The quotation:* A hundred years ago, the German philosopher Friedrich Nietzsche remarked that when God dies, culture becomes "weightless." When I first read that, I was deeply moved for three reasons.

First, weightlessness is a powerful biblical theme because it is the precise opposite of glory.

The glory of God is far more than his renown or radiance. Glory is God's own inexpressible reality, a reality so real that it alone has gravity and weight—the only "really real reality" in the entire universe. Therefore, when things move away from God, they become hollow and weightless, and we can accurately say, "Ichabod" ("The glory has departed"—1 Sam 4:21). Like Belshazzar (Dan 5:25-28), we read the handwriting on the wall: *Mene mene tekel u-pharsin* ("You are weighed in the balance and found weightless or wanting"). That's why idols, by contrast with God, are literally "nothings." That's why revival is the refilling of a nation with "the knowledge of the glory of the LORD as the waters fill the sea" (Hab 2:14).

Second, I was moved because Nietzsche was addressing his remarks to England, my homeland, at a time when most things appeared well both for the church and the nation. But Nietzsche had looked below the surface and seen the hollowing out that had begun. A generation characterized by "convictions" had been followed by one of "conventions" and was soon to be followed by one of "addictions." National greatness was in fact being hollowed out before World War I dealt it an irrecoverable blow. England was growing weightless from the inside.

Third, I was moved because many observers say that the eighties are America's weightless years—a second Gilded Age. True, Walt Whitman spoke of American hollowness a century ago, but for obvious reasons, such as America's prominence in the world and the strong persistence of faith, the process was arrested. But in the Reagan years, from families and schools to Wall Street boardrooms and Cabinet dealings, there have been widespread signs of weightlessness, of emptiness of ideals, of the gap between rhetoric and reality—a loss of the real stuff that will keep beliefs strong, ethics decisive and a nation great. And again, the church shows many of the same signs of weightlessness that you see in the world. One of the basic reasons for this is a lack of engagement in society in ways that are spiritually realistic as well as socially relevant.

In sum, "church and society" is not just a large, abstract topic. It is not even just one key topic among many. It is the test-bed truth that reveals the character and health of all our truths. If we don't demonstrate Christian truths in the crucible of society, then, whatever we profess, they mean nothing. In other words, this is far more than a topic for the "socially aware" or the "spiritually concerned." When we come to grips with the topic of church and society, we come to grips with all the deep questions of worship and discipleship in the modern world.

The purpose of this pamphlet is to set out first principles and general guidelines. So let me lay out six foundation considerations that need to be burned into our minds and hearts as we engage in society today. Each is a pair of ideas whose two halves are closely linked to each other yet interdependent with the other pairs of ideas. First are two perspectives; second, two principles; third, two great deficiencies; fourth, two reminders of where we are today; fifth, two requirements in relation to society; and last, two requirements in relation to the Lord.

## Two Perspectives

All engagement in society requires or reveals an answer to the question, How do we see society? There is a tendency for us to oscillate from one type of viewpoint to another—one moment optimistic, the next pessimistic, and so on. But the view of society we find in the Scriptures is a bifocal vision. Society is always and everywhere two things at once: God's gift to us and the devil's gauntlet thrown down before us, to challenge us to worship him and not Christ.

On the one hand, society is God's gift to us. To be sure, in comparison with what it might have been if there had been no Fall and what it will be when Christ comes again, what we see today is marred by evil, filled with pain and ruined with brokenness. Yet even when we have looked evil full in the face, we still know that society is God's gift. God is as decisive in sustaining society as society is decisive in shaping us. Only when we remember the former do we prevent the latter from becoming a fatalism that unnerves us.

Many Christians have forgotten both these truths, and modern individualism is a big reason why. Sin has always pivoted on the claim to the right to oneself, along with the accompanying claim to the right to see things from one's own point of view. Modern individualism therefore bolsters the pretense that we don't need others in any profound way.

But as biblical people, we should know that individualism is a dangerous illusion. We are social people willy nilly. We are who we are because we have grown up face to face. We live, work and play side by side. It is therefore important to us that God decisively sustains the world that decisively shapes us. Despite its fallenness, society is still God's gift to us and we should be thankful.

On the other hand, society is also the devil's gauntlet. However much we experience wonder, love and joy in it, society is under alien rule. Society is part of the first of the big trio—the world, the flesh and the devil. Thus, however much it is God's gift, society also contains a spirit, a system and a structure that stands over against the kingdom of God and his Christ.

Yes, the devil failed once. Out there in the desert, he promised everything, but God's great advocate overcame God's great adversary, and the devil left the field licked.

But the devil knows that where he failed with the Master, he may succeed with the servants. So he comes to us, and he invites us to enter and enjoy society at every level, from our work to our play, from the humblest levels up to the boardrooms of the country. "All this is yours," he says, "if only . . ." Buried in his invitation are the questions, Who is Lord? Have we faced up to the nature of the system? "Pick it up," says the Evil One. "All is yours . . . if you worship me."

Society, in other words, is the devil's gauntlet thrown down before us to induce us toward his lordship rather than Christ's. But that is not because we are the innocents and the world is tempting. Rather, we are the temptable ones. The world is simply our hearts writ large. Our hearts are simply the world writ small. So our view of society needs to be deeply realistic. If society is God's gift to us, it is also the devil's gauntlet and that bifocal vision should shape our perspective.

**Two Principles**

After the question, How do we see the world? comes a second one, How do we *act* in the world? Two great master principles have characterized the church at its most penetrating. The first is the Protagonist Principle which flows from the theme, "Christ *over* all" and has as its key word *total*.

The story of the exodus provides an Old Testament example. The whole issue with Pharaoh was lordship. He who can liberate is lord. As the contest and bargaining goes on, Pharaoh relents enough to let the Israelite men go, at least for worship. No, says Moses. "Let my people go" means not just the men and not just for worship. Men, women and children must go, and for good. And then a remarkable little phrase is added: "Not a hoof must be left behind" (Ex 10:26).

A New Testament example can be found in Luke 5. Peter, as fisherman, was glad to allow Jesus to preach from his boat. But then Jesus says to Peter, "Launch out into the deep and let down your nets on the other side."

You can almost hear Peter reply: "Look, Lord, I'll listen to you as teacher all day long, but when it comes to fishing, that's my job."

We know the result. Peter found that Jesus was Lord of nature too, and he could only say, "Depart from me, *Lord,* for I am a sinful man." Christ is Lord of nature as well as truth. He is the Alpha and the Omega. He is the source, guide and goal of all there is. That is why every eye will one day see him, every tongue will be stopped and every knee will bow. After all, as Abraham Kuyper said, expressing the Protagonist Principle perfectly, "There is not an inch of any sphere of life of which Jesus Christ the Lord does not say, 'Mine.' "

The second principle is the Antagonist Principle. It flows from the theme, "Christ *over against* all that does not bow to him." Here the key word is *tension.* The Lord himself puts the point unmistakably in the Ten Commandments: "I am the LORD your God . . . You shall have no other god to set against me" (Ex 20:2-3). Over forty times in Leviticus 18 and the following chapters there is a recurring assertion, "I am the LORD." Each time it introduces a strict instruction not to do as the Egyptians or the Canaanites did, neither following their idols nor copying their ideas and institutions.

The reason? The Lord is the jealous one, the one who brooks no rivals. Since he is our "decisive other," he demands of us a decisive contrast with everything that is over against him and his ways. And most wonderful of all, the deepest reason is not puritanical, but personal. It is "that you may belong to me."

In short, God and the world stand crosswise. We are in the world, but not of it. To be faithful to him, we have to be foreign to the world. We are not to be conformed, but transformed by the renewing of our minds.

Of course, the Protagonist Principle and the Antagonist Principle must never be separated. They go hand in hand. Without the Protagonist Principle the Antagonist Principle would create a we/they division. But the Protagonist Principle means there is no hatred of the world or false asceticism here. Yes, the world is passing away, and we are passing through the world. But, in the memorable phrase of Peter Berger, we are only *"against* the world *for* the world."

**Two Deficiencies**
The third foundation consideration grows from the question, Where has our engagement with the world gone wrong? Here we have to face the fact that under the conditions of the modern world, or what is called "modernity," a key breakdown between faith and obedience has occurred, one which is proving lethal to Christian integrity and effectiveness.

The full explanation of this breakdown is complicated.[1] Let me simply say that its roots are not only theological, but philosophical, sociological and spiritual. As a result of a whole combination of things, two glaring deficiencies in our discipleship have grown common.

First, as modern followers of Christ, we constantly face a peculiar temptation to break the link between belief and behavior. Anyone who wants to observe religion in the modern world and find the sort of belief that behaves would be advised to look at the cults rather than at Christians. What cult members believe may be bizarre, and the way they behave even worse, but to their credit there is a consistency between their belief and their behavior which is rare in the modern world.

Some years ago the Queen of the Belgians visited Poland. She went to Mass one day, accompanied by a government official. Noticing that he seemed to know a lot about the Catholic liturgy, she turned to him and asked, "Are you a Catholic?"

The official, looking embarrassed, replied, "Believing, Madam. Not practicing, I'm afraid."

"Oh, of course," she said, "you must be a Communist."

"Not exactly," he said, "Practicing, not believing, I'm afraid."

In other words, the breakdown between belief and behavior is not only an evangelical or even a Christian problem. It has affected almost all beliefs, though it hits us harder as Christians because of our specially strong claims as to what faith requires.

There has been considerable discussion recently about "cafeteria Catholicism"—mix your own morals, choose your own church, pick your own preference and so on. ("Yes, we love the Pope, but we don't follow his teaching.") But if there is a "cafeteria Catholicism," there is equally an "easy-care evangelicalism," and both are a result of the breakdown between believing and behaving.

A simple example is popular evangelical theology, some of the sloppiest and most superficial sentiment that has ever passed for theology. I cited an incident in *The Gravedigger File* that many people thought I had made up. In fact, it was true.

It came from watching a few minutes of a program on the electronic church. A Black singer sang an old spiritual in a way which threatened to inject reality into the proceedings. But the show's hostess clapped her hands, rolled her eyes heavenward and cooed, "Fantastic, brother! Fantastic! Christianity is so fantastic—who cares whether or not it's true?"

That incident was a few years ago, and many readers took it as purely funny. But after the scandalous revelations of 1987, the consequences of such corrupt theology in the lives of Jim and Tammy Faye Bakker have proved to be no joke.

Milder everyday examples are common. Not long ago, the call to worship in our church, a leading center of Episcopal renewal, went like this: "Come with me, walk with me, run with me, fly with me. We will roam the Father's land together. . . . Feeling the warmth of the sun about, we will know the loveliness of every hour."

A little earlier, I was in one of Washington's leading evangelical Presbyterian churches which had as its confession, "Father, forgive us for we have not lived up to our dreams." From the Hallmark-card theology of a thousand churches to the nauseating nonsense of PTL, American evangelicalism is awash in a sloppy, sentimental, superficial theology that wouldn't empower a clockwork mouse, let alone a disciple of Christ in the tough, modern world.

The second deficiency in discipleship concerns the broken link between the private world and the public world, through which faith becomes "privately engaging, but socially irrelevant."

The clearest example I know came during a *New York Times* interview with a celebrated business leader who was also a Christian. Asked what he believed in, he replied, "I believe in God, the family, and McDonald's hamburgers. And when I get to the office, I reverse the order."

Let's trust he was being facetious in a manner not picked up in the printed interview. But even if he was, he was only saying what millions of Christians do every single day without realizing it. Their faith flourishes at home, at church, in the prayer breakfasts before work or in the Bible study group during the lunch hour. But work itself is a different world, with a different way of doing things. Without realizing it, millions of Christians hang their faith along with their hats and coats at the door. The link between the private world of faith and the public world of work is severed.

It is true that there are magnificent exceptions to this problem. It is also true that both these deficiencies are offset by reactions that head in the opposite direction. For example, if one general problem in the church is *permissiveness* ("Anything goes"), some Christians have veered to the opposite extreme—a new kind of *particularism*. They see only one particular way as *the* Christian way of doing things—with the added insult that if you don't do it that way, you must not be a Christian.

Or again, if one general problem is the *privatization* of faith, some Christians have recently swung to the other extreme—*politicization*. They act as if politics in general and Washington in particular were the be-all and end-all of Christian obedience.

Both those errors, particularism and politicization, are a dangerous trap for disciples. But it is still the case that the opposite problems—permissiveness and not particularism, privatization and not politicization—are the greater problems for evangelicalism as a whole.

Dostoevsky's celebrated saying, "When God is dead, everything is permitted," could well be equally translated in America, "When God is dead, nothing is owed." For a characteristic of modern America is the absence of obligation. We owe nothing to anyone, except to ourselves. Words mean little, and bind no one. Therefore a deep danger of evangelicalism is that, even as we trumpet our concern for biblical authority, we reveal the disappearance of the Bible's "binding address." The Scriptures still address us in general but no longer bind us to anything in particular.

**Two Reminders**
The fourth pair of foundational considerations grows from the question, What is the setting in which we are discussing these questions? Clearly

we are not raising these questions in a vacuum or in a purely academic environment. Nor are we living in a great age of faith, such as the Reformation or the first Great Awakening.

Our cultural situation adds an urgent reminder to our discussion at two points. On the one hand, the United States is at a turning point, principally because of the decreasing influence of faith on society. On the other hand, the church is at a turning point, principally because of an increasing influence of society on faith.

I believe that the year 1986 will turn out to be the ironic parallel for conservatives of the year 1968 for liberals. In 1968, liberals hailed victory. For the first time, there was a solid majority against the Vietnam war. In fact, they were right: the majority was against the war. But it was also against liberals. It was Nixon's "emerging new majority." Thus 1968 was both the high point and a turning point, after which the tide flowed relentlessly against them.

In like manner 1986 may well prove to be the same for the conservatives. The Statue of Liberty celebrations in July saw the high tide of the claims for the conservative revolution. Now, just a few years later, most of those claims are in tatters. The conservative counter-revolution, like the liberal revolution before it, has been betrayed by its own illusions and inner contradictions.

This means that the period we are entering is

one of decisive reckoning because the United States is approaching the close of a generation-long crisis of cultural authority. After the great sixties' lurch in directions liberal, radical and secular came the great eighties' counter-lurch in directions conservative, traditional and religious. Now, with the failure of both revolutions on their own terms, we enter the showdown years that will reveal which faiths, which world views and which moral principles are going to prove decisive in shaping the nation over the next generations. The nation is at a turning point because of a decreasing influence of faith.

But we can see equally plainly that the church is at a turning point because of an increasing influence of culture. Americans used to speak much of their "exceptionalism." Today there is only one place left where America is still exceptional—the strength of religion. In a world in which modernity and secularity seem to go hand in hand, the U.S. is simultaneously the most modern and the most religious of modern countries. Yet with the striking discrepancy between indicators (church attendance, giving, praying) and the social influence—the former up and the latter down—the exception cannot continue for long. There is too little religion and too much religiosity in the church. The church's showdown period is beginning too, when its true integrity and effectiveness will be revealed.

**Two Requirements before the World**

The fifth pair of foundational considerations is an answer to the question, What do we most need as we engage with our society? Let me suggest two things that relate to our public witness—the need for a Christian mind and a public philosophy.

In 1976 *(Newsweek's* "Year of the Evangelical") many observers asked whether the evangelical community would make the impact which its history, numbers and opportunity might lead one to expect. The answer was generally no, and the main reason given was that evangelicals were unlikely to think in any distinctively Christian way.

Such predictions have proved lamentably correct. Failure to "think Christianly" is the Achilles' heel of English-speaking evangelicalism. While the Puritans were magnificently different, evangelicals since the Great Awakening have by and large displayed only a "ghost mind," hollowed out by various forces which for all their spiritual passion led toward a general anti-intellectualism. Since then, with exceptions only proving the rule, there has been no powerful evangelical mind. Thus at most of the decisive moments in American thinking— Emerson's "intellectual Declaration of Independence" at Harvard in 1837, the rise of higher education and of liberalism, and so on—evangelicals were not so much out-thought as out of it. And they still are today.

When will we face the fact that our deep-rooted

anti-intellectualism is worse than ineffective? It is sub-Christian, disobedient, antispiritual and unloving. Only when we root out the last traces of it can we hope to exercise the public influence that faithfulness to Christ demands. For in the end, thinking Christianly has nothing to do with being intellectual. God forbid. It is a matter of faithfulness and loving God.

Let me be specific. Since living here in Washington the past few years, the single spiritual lesson that I have benefited from most is the reminder of our grand priority: that above all else we are to love the Lord with all our heart, soul, strength and mind. Christ himself and not "Christianity" is our first love, our primary call, our fundamental loyalty.

I confess that I needed that reminder, and I have benefited from adjusting to that priority. So I thank God for it, but to be candid, I am saddened by the selectiveness of what it means around Washington. There are all too many who love the Lord with all their hearts, soul and strength, but leave out their "minds" from the list. Under the guise of an ostensibly spiritual priority, they rationalize the plain disobedience of anti-intellectualism. Unless this generation of American evangelicals confronts its centuries-old habit of anti-intellectualism, we don't have the slightest chance of penetrating modern society for Christ.

The second external requirement is a contribution to America's public philosophy that has both Christian integrity and public credibility. The United States has always been characterized by its astonishing blend of liberty, diversity and harmony. Put differently, consensus-building has become one of America's greatest achievements and special needs. Despite such diversity, consensus maintains unity. Despite change, it maintains continuity. It is this common vision of the common good that Walter Lippman called the "public philosophy."

Obviously, a key part of this public philosophy has been an agreed understanding of the place of religion in public life and of the guiding principles within which citizens with religious differences can contend with each other in the public square. But equally obviously, if the public philosophy is in poor shape today, this particular part is in chronic disrepair.

Look at the controversies over religion and politics in the last ten years. Debates have been fruitlessly polarized, issues dominated by the extremes, resolution has been sought reflexively from the courts, the two religious liberty clauses of the First Amendment to the Constitution have been pitted against each other, and there has been an evident breakdown of any shared understanding of how religiously grounded differences should be negotiated in the public square. Worst of all, evangelicals and fundamentalists have often made the problems worse. With their better voices unheard, and those heard relying solely on a confrontational style and being concerned solely with "me/my/our" interests, they too have caused great damage to the public philosophy.

There are deeper issues here than we have space to explore. But let me simply state that we need to be heard to say, "Christian justice is not justice for Christians. It is justice for everybody." Rights are universal and responsibilities mutual; so a right for one is a right for another and a responsibility for both. A right for a Protestant is a right for a Catholic, is a right for a Jew, is a right for a humanist, is a right for a Mormon and a right for the believer of any faith under God's wide heaven.

The First Amendment in this sense is the epitome of public justice and serves as the Golden Rule for civic life: rights are best protected and responsibilities best exercised if we guard for others those rights we would wish guarded for ourselves.

Beyond the principled reasons for a public philosophy are pragmatic ones. The recent contentious debates, at least in their high-octane form, are not likely to continue forever. War-weariness is already setting in. The public is tired of the trench warfare over religion and public life. But if we are not careful, the danger is of a great sea change in public attitudes. Instead of faith and freedom being viewed as blood brothers, as they have been for two hundred years, they will come to be viewed as in opposing corners—with titanic implications for the gospel and for the nation.

## Two Requirements before the Lord

The last pair of foundational considerations concerns two requirements that we need before the Lord. If we ask what it is we most need, the answer in two words is: God himself. But let me just draw out two simple requirements—a proclamation of the Word and a visitation of the Spirit. They need stressing because they are so simple that we easily overlook them.

President Lyndon Johnson used to tell a story of a preacher who prepared a stirring but rather complicated sermon that required notes. Unfortunately on his way to church he dropped the notes, and they were eaten by a dog. Unabashed he climbed into the pulpit and said, "Brothers and sisters, I'm afraid a dog ate my sermon notes on the way to church. I'm just going to have to rely on what the Holy Spirit tells me, but I promise I'll do better next week."

That may be closer to the situation in many American pulpits than many Americans realize. Having visited almost all the countries in the English-speaking world, I would say that I know none where the churches are more full and the sermons more empty than in America. There are magnificent exceptions, of course. But by and large, I am never hungrier and rarely angrier than when I come out of an American evangelical church after what passes for the preaching of the Word of God.

The problem is not just the heresy, though doubtless there is some of that. Nor is it just the degree of entertainment, and there is lots of that. Nor is it even the appalling gaps in the theology, for there is far too much of that. The real problem is that in what is said there is almost no sense of announcement from God; and in what is shown, there is almost no sense of anointing by God.

Jeremiah attacked the false prophets of his day with the damning question, "Which of them has stood in the council of the LORD, seen him and heard his word?" (Jer 23:18). Are we who profess a high view of authority much better in practice? Is such a standard too demanding? I admit that my own expectations have been shaped decisively by the standards common when I came to Christ. As a student I had the privilege of sitting under the ministry of Martyn Lloyd-Jones at his greatest. Before he preached every Sunday, he was alone for an hour with the Lord. Nobody disturbed him. If the prime minister had arrived, someone else could greet him. If a person in crisis had come, somebody else could counsel them. The pastor was with the King of kings. I don't remember Dr. Lloyd-Jones ever saying, "Thus saith the Lord."

He didn't have to. His very bearing, quite apart from his words, bespoke that what he said was an announcement from God given with the anointing of God.

Loss of proclamation goes wider than preaching. Christian discourse in general is suffering. As part of our overall secularization we have shifted from a proclamation style to a discussion style, and the result is an endless proliferation of consultations, forums, seminars, symposiums, congresses, workshops. In most cases, old-fashioned proclamation would seem about as appropriate in those affairs as a full-throated obscenity, and no more likely.

The second requirement is a visitation of the Spirit. I use the old Puritan word *visitation* deliberately, because so many of the words describing revival have been devalued. We have no need of religious *resurgence,* because that word is used of trends that are explicable in purely social terms. Nor can we be content to use the word *revival* merely as a synonym for evangelism. And *visitation* is far beyond what is usually called *renewal.* I am personally in favor of the renewal movement at its best, particularly where it touches personal worship and musical forms. But even at its best, the renewal movement is a million miles short of true revival. Where is its note of profound conviction? Where is the wholesale changing of communities? Where is the developed passion for social holiness, as opposed to personal devotion?

Sadly, revival raises a question to many evangelicals: Do they believe in it still? Two years ago, Paul Weyrich, a leading conservative strategist, gave a speech called "Taking Stock." In it he argued in effect, "Even if we conservatives win our entire agenda, we've lost." He shocked his audience further. "Yes," he said, "abortion, school prayer . . . win them all, and we will still have failed." Why? Because social change has changed too much, political change can change too little. Culture is flowing away faster than any piecemeal action can remedy. Nothing short of a total cultural transformation of America will do.

Curiously, evangelicals a generation ago would have taken that as a truism. But in a day when political activism is in vogue, many who used to pray confidently, realistically and practically for revival no longer have that hunger for a visitation from God.

### Show Me Your Glory

Let me draw the threads together. Review these six foundational themes in the setting of your own life and that of your local church. Are those two perspectives burnt into your mind, those two principles mastering your life, those two deficiencies highlighted so that you can avoid them, those two reminders spurring you on, and those two requirements before the world and the Lord being met? I imagine you feel like many of us. Who is equal to the challenge? Can we really expect to see our culture turned around in our day?

Questions like those make me think of two men under pressure. One was the great German thinker Max Weber. He never shut his eyes to the modern world. He wrestled with it, but the more he wrestled, the more pessimistic he became. One day a friend saw him pacing up and down, nearing the verge of a second breakdown.

"Max," he said, "why do you go on thinking like this when your conclusions leave you so depressed?"

Weber's reply has become a classic of intellectual commitment and courage: "I want to see how much I can stand."

Admirable in many respects, that is not the way for followers of Christ. We are not called to be tragic heroes, or stoics or spiritual masochists.

A very different response under pressure was that of Moses. Faced by enemies behind, around and ahead, and finding discontent not only among his own people but within his own family, he suddenly met the ultimate threat to his people and his task as leader: God himself. The Lord declared that he would destroy the Israelites himself because of their sin.

His very life and trust in God called into question, Moses stood firm and countered the challenge by putting God on the line (arguing the covenant), the people on the line (calling for a consecration to the Lord even against families and friends) and finally himself on the line (asking that he himself rather than the people be blotted out).

Then, when the Lord had listened to his prayers, agreeing first to forgive the people and then to come with them in person, rather than by an angel, Moses made his supreme request, surely the most audacious prayer in all the Scriptures: "Show me thy glory" (Ex 33:18). He wanted to know all of God that a fallen sinner could be allowed to know, for nothing less would be enough to see him through.

In that prayer we have our answer to Nietzsche. When God "dies" for a nation, a church or an individual, a weightlessness results for which there is only one remedy—the glory of God refilling them as the waters fill the sea. Wasn't that Jeremiah's message to his generation? To a people who had exchanged their glory for a god altogether nothing, he warned, "Ascribe glory to the LORD before the darkness falls" (Jer 13:16).

G. K. Chesterton, the great Christian apologist, brought the same message to the United States after his visit in 1921. The glory of the American republic, he argued, had not been derived from itself and could not be sustained by itself. Cut off from the source from which it sprang, it would not long endure. He then concluded his book with the magnificent line: "Freedom is the eagle whose glory is gazing at the sun."

If we today stress the spiritual aspects of the gospel without the social, we lose all relevance in modern society. But if we stress the social without the spiritual, we lose our reality altogether. The ultimate factor in the church's engagement with society is the church's engagement with God.

Are we still tempted today to believe that we or anyone else can pull things around? We must forget it. On the other hand, are we overwhelmed by the task, overburdened by the state of the nation and the world? For God's sake, let us forget the eagle and ourselves and turn with Moses to the sun: "Lord, show me your glory."

## Notes

[1]I have discussed this in more detail in *The Gravedigger File* (Downers Grove, Ill: InterVarsity Press, 1983).